LET'S PLAY
OUTDOORS

LET'S PLAY OUTDOORS

Prepared by

KATHERINE READ BAKER

*Assisted by members
of the Nursery School Staff,
Oregon State University,
Corvallis, Oregon*

Revised Edition

National Association for the Education of Young Children

1629 21st Street, N.W., Washington, D.C. 20009

Publications Committee
NATIONAL ASSOCIATION FOR THE EDUCATION OF YOUNG CHILDREN
Chairman: Lucile Perryman, Queens College
Evelyn Beyer, Sarah Lawrence College
Mary Moffit, Queens College
Eveline Omwake, Connecticut College

NAEYC Publication #101 ● Price: $1.00

Library of Congress Catalog Card Number: AC66-10181

THIRD PRINTING, JUNE 1967

CONTENTS

PHOTOGRAPHERS

Robert L. Beckhard, New York City

Pages x, 2, 15, 29, 31, 35

Donna J. Harris, The Merrill-Palmer Institute, Detroit, Michigan

Pages 3, 6, 8, 12–13, 21, 22–23, 24–25, 28, 32–33

Images-by-Kamen, Cold Spring Harbor, New York

Cover; Pages 4, 5, 7, 9, 11, 16, 17, 19, 20, 26–27, 30, 34

Suzanne Szasz, New York City

Page 10

INTRODUCTION

Katherine Read Baker is a widely recognized pioneer in the field of early childhood education. For some 25 years, as a college professor, she has guided the thinking of countless teachers and students, helping them gain greater insight into the special world of the young child.

Dr. Baker is internationally known for her book *The Nursery School: A Human Relationships Laboratory.* The fact that it is now in its fourth revision and that it has been translated into Danish, Japanese, Hebrew, and Swedish attests to the lasting significance of this book.

Katherine Baker's accent has always been on the understanding of child behavior. This revised pamphlet *Let's Play Outdoors* is no exception. Its many suggestions for outdoor experiences will help teachers in re-thinking their programs so as to provide a richer learning environment for young children. At a time when nursery and kindergarten teachers are focusing their attention on formal learning confined to the classroom, Dr. Baker here re-affirms the child's need and right to learn from the wider world outside.

Lucile C. Perryman, *Chairman*
Publications Committee
National Association for the
Education of Young Children

March, 1966

Let's play outdoors!

The nursery school teacher uses these words often and hears them many times from the children. They are important words. They remind us of how much outdoor play means in the life of the nursery school age child. In providing plenty of outdoor play space and outdoor equipment the nursery school is offering children essential living and learning experiences.

For many children today outdoor play space at home is limited —for children in apartment buildings, in crowded housing units, on narrow city lots. Yet every child needs the feel of wind and sun against his cheeks, the tickle of grass between his bare toes, the smell of fresh earth as he digs, the sight of blossoms drifting from the trees or of leaves falling. Every child needs freedom to run without thought of traffic dangers and freedom to climb on something more acceptable and satisfying than furniture. He needs to find these things in the good nursery school.

As teachers, we must make sure that the nursery school offers children opportunities for rich play experience outside. We must ask ourselves some questions. What kind of planning can we do for outdoor play? How can we contribute toward making the outdoor play richer and more satisfying for the child?

Every child needs the feel of the sun and wind on his cheek, and a time for quiet wonder.

THE PLAY AREA

Plenty of Space

A first consideration in planning will be to see that there is ample play space outside. We must not be content with a tiny corner barren of play possibilities or we will find children losing interest in playing outdoors. We may be in the position of the teacher who said, "My group doesn't like to go outdoors." Space is the first requirement—space which can be filled with rich possibilities by a resourceful teacher.

The number of square feet of space needed per child cannot be stated exactly because many factors influence the figure. The most useful arrangement is when the outdoor space is adjacent to the indoor space, with easy access to the toilet room. When the two play areas are adjacent, teaching time is not spent in the relatively unprofitable task of supervising children as they go back and forth. Greater flexibility in program is possible when indoor space opens directly on to the outdoor space. Equipment can be used in both areas more easily. Children themselves find it easier to go outside.

A Fence

We will want a fence around the playground as another important requirement. If the fence is substantial, sufficiently high and constructed in such a way that does not invite climbing, with child-proof exits, it reduces the problems of supervision. It

A fence should be substantial, sufficiently high, and with child-proof exits.

Semi-sheltered areas provide cover
from sun as well as rain.

gives children the security of safe limits for which they are not held responsible. It leaves them free. It relieves teachers of anxiety and frees them, too, to do a more profitable kind of teaching than that of patrol duty.

Sunshine and Shade

The area should have shade as well as sun. Trees which give shade in the warm weather, but do not take away from the sunshine available in the winter, are a real advantage. Shelter from the prevailing winds may take the form of a long covered play "shed" or passageway which can be used for outdoor play on rainy, cold days. A covered outdoor area, large enough for active play, is especially important in climates where there are many rainy days without extremely cold temperatures. The restlessness of a rainy day is offset by a chance to play outdoors.

Landscaping

Children enjoy the privacy which carefully considered landscaping can give. Shrubs may be planted to make a corner where a group engaged in housekeeping play can withdraw without being entirely removed from the watchful eye of the teacher. But the shrubbery or the fence should not hide from the children too much of what is going on around them. Children take an active interest in the sights and sounds of the world outside the school. They should be encouraged to look when they are interested. A high solid fence or thick shrubbery prevents them from satisfying this interest. Good landscaping should give them privacy and protection from the weather, yet not prevent them from seeing what passes the play area.

Hardy plants, both evergreen and deciduous, that provide different types of flowers through a long blooming season and distribute seeds in a variety of ways can offer the nursery school child a breadth of learning about the world of plants.

Variety in Surfacing

Besides being safe, with sunshine and shade and protection from the weather, the outdoor space for children will meet other requirements. It will have more than one kind of surfacing. Grass is the most "natural" outdoor surface and lends itself to many types of play activities. Even though rubbers must often be used when the child goes outside to play on a grassy area, grass offers enough in satisfaction to overcome this disadvantage. Some of the outdoor play space should be covered with grass if possible. The climbing equipment may well be placed in this area. It's not so hard to tumble on grass!

Part of the outdoor area, however, should have a hard surface for play in wet weather and for play with wheel toys. It should be well drained and some of it, at least, covered with a surfacing like tanbark, asphalt or pavement. Concrete is probably the most satisfactory for use with wheel toys. We should plan for a hard-surfaced area because wheel toys are of such importance in the play life of the preschool child. Incidentally, in laying out a walk

Hardy evergreens and deciduous plants can provide the child a breadth of learning about the world of plants

A good outdoor area provides a variety of surfacing—grass, tanbark, asphalt or pavement.

Digging gives pleasure and a sense of accomplishment.

or concrete area on the playground, we are too likely to use right angled corners because we are conditioned to sidewalks and streets with right angles. Instead we should take our cue from the highway engineer and plan for curves. Traffic on wagons and tricycles is often fast traffic and easily becomes congested. Walks with rounded curves handle this traffic more easily. A paved circle around the playground and perhaps a large paved area at some convenient point for parking, backing, and group play may meet our needs most satisfactorily.

Some kind of inclined surface adds to the possibilities of the playground. In a flat yard this may be a wooden ramp sloping on both sides for wagons and tricycles to speed downhill. In some playgrounds the land itself will offer a chance to experiment with slopes. When the sidewalks were laid in one school, the dirt was piled in a corner of the yard to make a "hill." This "hill" became a favorite play spot for the children.

A Digging Area

A digging area also has an important place in our planning. The earth holds many secrets for children to discover—roots, stones, worms, buried treasure of many kinds. Digging with a short handled shovel gives satisfaction to most three- and four-year-olds. The sense of accomplishment as the hole gets bigger, the effort it takes to overcome the resistant ground, may help relieve the burden that some anxious, hostile children carry. In wet weather the digging area becomes a mud hole, the kind of place that children eagerly seek, where they may find the sensory satisfaction they crave as release from the demands to be clean which we civilized people make on ourselves. Children find it easier to face these demands if they can escape from them for a time in a good old mud hole! It may take an alert teacher to give them this freedom and yet protect their health, (no sitting down in wet holes, boots on, etc.) while she also takes some responsibility for clothing; but every playground is better off for having a digging area even though the landscape gardeners may protest. At times this area will be transformed by the children into a garden area with a strange variety of plants. But the digging area should not be part of the formal garden—even though formal planting may also play an important part in making the environment attractive and interesting.

EQUIPMENT AND EXPERIENCES

This is our playground. How shall we equip it? What kinds of experiences are children seeking as they play here?

The Importance of Large Muscle Activities

We might describe the preschool child as a child in the large muscle stage of development. He is the climbing-wheel-toy child, engrossed in perfecting his large muscle coordinations. Having

Every child needs the freedom
to run, climb and slide, without
danger to himself and others.

"Watch me go fast!"

struggled to pull himself to a standing position, he continues his
progress by looking for ways to climb higher and higher. Having
mastered the art of walking, he delights in running and in riding
fast. Having acquired the ability to drop an object at will, he is
ready to try throwing. He pulls and pushes. He is gaining motor
skill and strength and growing rapidly. In using his large muscle
the child is easy and comfortable and free of the strain which
comes when he uses his fine muscles. Through his motor accom-
plishments he is laying part of the basic pattern of self confidence
he needs. He is developing greater capacity to meet problems
and to get together with others of his own age.

The child who rides a tricycle with skill meets other children.
His motor skills "count" in the world of childhood. They help
him win a place for himself. He "belongs" with others and feels
secure. To run with confidence, to climb easily, to keep one's
balance, are abilities worth a lot in the life of the preschooler,
worth much more than the ability to recognize letters or name
colors! Outdoor play offers the nursery school child these important values.

Jimmy, for example, was a child of elderly parents. Life in his
comfortable home had been filled with listening to music or to
stories and quiet play with small blocks or coloring books. When
he first came to nursery school, he retreated from the active
world in which the children lived. He sat by the victrola and, if
given a choice, would politely refuse to go outside. He didn't
care for swinging or climbing or running or jumping—and the
children didn't find him fun. After some time the rhythm of

"Up here, I can feel
as big as a giant!"

swinging seemed to attract him and very slowly he began playing more actively and gaining some motor skills. With skill came confidence and contacts with other children. Jimmy had attended nursery school nearly six months before he could bring himself to try going down the slide. His delight when he succeeded was evident. He used the slide again and again, squealing with joy, calling everyone's attention to his accomplishment. His growth was rapid from this time on. He began to stand up for himself in play. His tenseness diminished and his friendliness increased. He grew more child-like and more of a person in his own right. It had taken him a long time to enjoy the outdoors but when he discovered himself there, he could grow as a child.

Climbing

A slide is always a delight, especially if it is not too high so that children can use it with confidence and the sense of being safe. A jungle gym is another piece of equipment found on most playgrounds. It offers many climbing possibilities. If the child climbs without urging, he is safe for he is likely only to go as high as he feels sure he can handle himself. The teacher's part is to stand close and see that there is no pushing or interference by one child with another when two or more are climbing.

The jungle gym is rich in dramatic possibilities, too. Alan had been to the zoo. He played the jungle gym was a monkey house and he was the monkey. Bonnie and Gay called it the jail and locked each other up in it. They played they were safe there from

Barrels are fun, too!

a big giant! Sometimes the jungle gym becomes a boat where a group rides safely above the water. Or children fish from its height, holding long strings which trail on the grass. Sometimes it is a fire station from which they climb down to speed to imaginary fires. Sometimes it becomes an airplane high above the earth.

Another satisfactory way to provide climbing experiences with the maximum of safety is by a platform, perhaps five feet off the ground, with a solid railing of rungs close together around the top and a variety of ways of climbing on and off the platform. One approach can be a stairway which gives step climbing practice to the younger children and enables any of them to take their dolls and housekeeping materials up on the platform. A vertical fixed ladder, a swinging rope ladder, a pole "like the firemen have," perhaps a slide, may form part of this piece of large equipment. The space underneath may be used for storage, especially if it is enclosed. The children usually prefer to play on top where they can look down on the world and the adults in it. If the platform is placed where there is shade in the summer, it becomes a tree house where the children seem to find escape from the limitations of being little and enjoy living off the ground, way up high. One group who enjoyed the platform used to play it was "church" and march solemnly up the stairs to sit up above the world. The combination of ladders on the side makes it a piece of equipment which challenges many levels of skill and develops coordination as well as imagination. Yet it remains a safe piece of equipment for children to use.

A simple wheel
becomes a ship:
"When will you
be back, Captain?"

Boxes, Boards and Barrels

Many other pieces of equipment promote large muscle development. Nothing, of course, takes the place of a small tree with low growing limbs in giving children a sense of achievement and the fun of being up among the leaves. Large saw horses with rungs on the side make an easy beginning climbing experience for the younger child. Packing boxes offer climbing possibilities as well as serving purposes in dramatic play. One child will make steps with blocks to reach the top of the box. Another will pull a board over and lean it against the top as a ramp for climbing. Even cardboard cartons are good for a morning of play outdoors, to be carried around, or to be combined with blocks for a house. Smooth varnished or painted boards of different lengths make a valuable addition to the playground equipment. One of their greatest values lies in the challenge they offer the children to set up new combinations for play. A board from a rung in the jungle gym makes a gentle incline or a steep one, depending on where it is placed. Short boards add interesting possibilities in block play. Long boards can be combined with saw horses to make walking boards or bouncing boards—if they are flexible and strong.

Barrels are fun too. Climbing into a barrel is a real feat for the child. Once there he can pop up like a jack-in-box. Rolling inside the barrel like the little pig in the story is possible if someone pushes. Barrels are fun to crawl through! Barrels can also be sawed in half and mounted on castors with a rope attached.

Then they become wagons for transporting materials or even people in the style of "three men in a tub." The children in one school enjoyed having a real pump (found in a second hand store) fastened to the top of a barrel. They loved to watch the water rush out of the spout and gurgle back into the barrel, or fill their dishes for the sand box. Pumping is good exercise, too!

Dramatic Play Outdoors

Many kinds of vigorous, dramatic play may be promoted outdoors by the right materials. A whole fire department may organize itself if there are short pieces of hose at hand and a small ladder or two. The play grows in complexity with some shovels, a wagon, and concepts coming from a trip to the nearest fire station to see the equipment there and meet the friendly firemen.

All of the wagons and pull type of toys may be put to use in the game of "moving." A group may work hard depositing all the movable equipment at one end of the yard, only to pile it on "trucks" and change the location to a new spot. They may need little help from the teacher outside of a steadying hand when the pile of blocks or household goods is high, a definition from her of what may be moved and some arbitration when cross purposes appear in the group. This is real group play at the preschool level. Working together in moving a pile of blocks from one place to another can be an experience in cooperation on the level at which the child is ready to cooperate and where he has a good chance of success.

What is so free as to
go up in a swing?

In a school located on a campus where mowing machines were used to cut the grass the children would go back and forth over the grass on their tricycles, chanting, "mowing, mowing the grass, mowing, mowing." They would get off the tricycles and carefully move the equipment, enlisting the aid of the teacher when the piece was too heavy, continuing until the job was done to their satisfaction.

Gardening

Short handled shovels and hoes make vigorous digging possible. Children enjoy gardening and even though the garden may be re-dug often, some plants usually manage to come up in time. One group of four-year-olds was successful in raising some carrots and peas one year. Great was their joy the day they had a "picnic" under the trees, enjoying tender peas from the pod and young carrots, freshly pulled and scrubbed. Food seemed to take on a new meaning for them.

Expressing Feelings Outdoors

There need to be opportunities for draining off negative feelings in play too. Outdoor play offers many possibilities. Throwing is likely to be more of a release, for example, if there is something to hit or hit against as a target or some type of "back stop." The side of a playshed where there are no windows may make a target for bean bags or balls. Throwing against the wall helps relieve aggressive feelings. One school had a wall back of the

sand box and sometimes a child would throw the wet sand against this in hard pats.

A punching bag on a stand is another outdoor possibility for release of aggressive feelings and it is convenient to use. A punching bag may also be fastened to a beam in the roof on a porch or playshed and to the floor for use when those "punching feelings" appear. Even a flour sack stuffed with cotton material or a heavier sack filled with sawdust serves this purpose.

Running and rolling and tussling with a huge rubber ball is another source of satisfaction and activity. A large truck inner tube, mentioned in another connection, has its uses here. An old mattress covered with a washable slip cover gives a safe place for rolling and for jumping, too. With straps the mattress can be hung out of the way on a wall when it is not in use.

Swinging and singing go together and many children such as Jimmy, mentioned previously, find satisfaction and expression as they swing and sing. But swings must be carefully supervised. Some schools enclose the swing area with rail fences. Only swingers may be inside. Such a mechanical barrier is an aid to the teacher and a protection to wandering children. Swings are best with soft seats of leather or fabric. Children must be prevented from running in front of swings, and pushing a child high may be dangerous when he is inexperienced in swinging. A swing suspended from three points instead of two makes it possible even for a two-year-old to swing himself. One school had two of these swings made by a local carpenter to resemble a horse with seat, head and rope tail. These swings were in almost constant use all year round, bringing many quiet children outdoors and into contact with a companion.

Using Large Blocks

Large blocks are an important part of the outside equipment in any nursery school. No playground is really complete without some outdoor blocks and small boxes and lengths of smooth boards. Blocks of waterproofed plywood in sizes about 4"x6"x12" can be made in a local cabinet shop. While they cannot be left out in the rain, they withstand the ordinary dampness of grass and ground. Many are the engineering feats possible with substantial blocks. Laid in a row they form a walk or a road. They may be used to make a house with high walls or one with rooms laid out in patterns. When the bunny needs a pen, it's easy to make him one with blocks so that he can be left free to hop around on the grass for part of the morning. Blocks can be carried, sat on, stood on, walked on and used as cargo for wagons and wheelbarrows. Building with large blocks is important in the development of muscles and the emotional satisfactions it gives as well as for the problem solving that develops from it.

At the Workbench

It is easy to realize why the work bench belongs outside under a covered shelter if possible. Even a few hammers at work make a lot of noise! With sturdy hammers, nails of different sizes (mostly with large heads), and scraps of soft wood, children

work in a sustained way at many levels of skill. On one playground the youngest children used an old tree stump in the yard to pound short, large headed nails into. When there was no more empty space on the stump, the teacher pulled out the nails and the project would begin again. These children were practicing and learning skills which will have much value for them someday. No one set them the task but they pursued it eagerly. Older children make boats, airplanes, anything by pounding two pieces of wood together. They enjoy the vise for the possibilities it offers in manipulation, but they soon learn to use it to hold the wood while they saw.

For some children there seems to be a great deal of satisfaction in attacking resistant material such as wood and cutting it in two. Anyone who has seen the joy on a three-year-old's face when his efforts are rewarded and he makes two pieces out of one cannot fail to appreciate the significance which such a mastery of materials has for a child. The teacher has an important role to play in making this possible. She must see that the saw is sharp and the wood soft. She must stand ready to forestall danger, to show the child where to place his hands, how to stand, and the proper use of the tool. She may need to do a little steering of the saw in the first attempts to keep the line straight, even to move the saw along with the child so that he may succeed and find the thrill that comes with success.

Constant supervision is essential at the workbench. Safety comes first. Tools must be used with respect and within limits. If the bench is one used by more than one child, the number of

children using it may need to be strictly limited. The situation must be kept simple enough so that it can be easily supervised and it must be kept under supervision at all times.

With larger pieces of wood and some help from the teacher, the older nursery school children can accomplish projects such as a pen for the chickens, a hutch for the rabbit, even a simple play house for themselves. Mixing cement, setting posts, making paths and even brick work are not beyond their level of skill if preschool standards of workmanship are accepted by the understanding teacher. Many a hostile child drains off some of his hostility as he attacks the wood. He discovers an outlet that is creative and satisfying. The wise teacher will see that such a child has plenty of opportunity to use a hammer and saw but she may stand between him and another child while he is working with tools like these.

Water Play Is Essential

Water play is also a valuable avenue of release for a tense or hostile child. It brings satisfaction to all healthy children too. Although it may seem difficult to provide, its value is so great that real thought needs to be given to seeing that children have some chance to play in water. In the summer time water play can be provided outdoors. The school with a wading pool is fortunate. Rubber rafts and Koroseal pools make wading places available for many more schools today. Children enjoy the splashing and endless experimenting with objects which water

page 21

Man the buckets—the ship is sinking!

invites. Playing in water is satisfying while the child is learning about things that float and things that don't, how to balance a cargo of blocks on a board, how to set up currents that carry floating leaves, about the difference in things when they are wet and dry, and many other learnings. Sometimes the sand box can be turned into a river with the hose. On cooler days a tub or table with metal pan inset may offer opportunities for play in water. Children love to wash doll clothes outside on sunny days and hang them up to dry. Or they enjoy giving their dolls a bath with sudsy water in a big tub. However we may achieve it, we should look for ways to give children experiences with water.

Even on cool days it may be possible to "paint" outdoors with water. Carrying a large can or small pail filled "not too full" of water and a man-sized paintbrush, the child can "paint" the outside equipment to his heart's content. Carolyn and Alice, each with a brush and a pail between them, painted the slide, talking as they worked, "I've got to get the utility room painted," and "Now I'll do the living room." Terry, Larry, and Tom had watched a paint crew at work. They played they were members of the crew. Each had a can of water and a brush. Terry pulled the wagon while Larry and Tom rode, sitting on the side of the wagon. They went from one piece of equipment to the next, jumping off to cover it with water paint. As they painted inside the storage shed, they remarked, "Just like a real house." Terry would say, "Come on, let's go," and the others would hurriedly pick up their cans, load them on the wagon, and move on. The play went on for more than half an hour. They said very little, not seeming to need conversation but working busily together on a common purpose and accepting each other.

Nothing Like Sand

The sand box holds such an important place in the nursery school play yard that it deserves to be discussed by itself. Children can enjoy sand many times when dirt and mud must be denied them as play materials. Sand is easily brushed off, yet wet or dry, it is a medium which leads to creativity and expression. Rows of "pies" and "cakes" may line one end of the box, baking in the sun, while the other end is full of roads and tunnels and trucks. Children at all stages of development turn to the sand box and find it offers them some type of activity. It brings quiet children together in parallel play—play which requires few adjustments and enables them to find success with others before they are ready to meet the social demands of more complex situations. As any teacher knows, the sand box can become a "hot spot" in social relations too. Conflicts over spoons and pans or space, interferences of many kinds lead to disputes. There are limits to be maintained. Sand must be kept in the box; it must not be thrown. But these are simple, clear cut rules. With the teacher's help, the children learn many social lessons in the sand box while they enjoy the untold possibilities sand offers as a creative medium.

Cans with smooth edges and a coat of bright paint, small muffin tins, large spoons, scoops, sifters, almost anything used in

A child needs to get into the sand himself—and live in it completely.

baking in the kitchen add richness and variety to the play. Kitchen equipment is not all that the child enjoys here. Small autos, trucks, especially those which dump materials, help him recreate other activities of interest to him. A sand table is not as satisfying to a child as sand in a box. He needs to get into the sand himself—to live in it more completely than is possible at a table. If the sand is damp, he can sit on a block to keep dry yet be inside the box. Some kind of cover is necessary to keep the sand clean. If the cover is made so that it folds back in sections (for ease in handling) and rests on a frame to keep it horizontal, it adds to the play surface available where cakes and pies can be put to bake and cars parked, etc. Many children start their outdoor play in the sand box when they enter nursery school, watching the more active play which goes on around them. As they feel more at home, they move on to other play interests but almost all children keep coming back to the sand box at intervals because of the satisfaction that play with sand brings.

Children Are Curious

Nursery school children are not only active, they are curious. They are exploring and experimenting with physical forces, using inclines for rolling things down or pushing things up, balancing on boards or teeters, using wheels of many kinds, pulleys and pumps and springs. As we enrich the outdoor play space, we may find ourselves turning it into something like a laboratory. We might think of one function of the playground as a set-up to provide children with experiences with physical forces. In an environment rich in experiences like these, children have more chance of understanding the world which depends to such an extent on a knowledge of physics. Anyone who has ever watched the variety in play which children develop when they use a bicycle pump, for example, would put such a pump ahead of most toys. Endless experiments with air currents and rich dramatic play are possible.

Second Hand Parts

Used parts of automobiles, old steering wheels, hub caps, different sizes of pipe with some large enough for children to crawl through or listen to the echo as they shout through them, plumbing supplies such as old faucets—these are all raw materials for play and for learning. They can be part of the outdoor equipment of the nursery school at little cost. The resourceful teacher, visiting second hand stores, will find many other possibilities. These raw materials encourage creative, dramatic play, play which calls for resourcefulness, effort, hard work; play that brings real satisfaction to children like David who sighed happily on leaving school, "We worked hard today, didn't we!"

A Truck Inner Tube

A truck inner tube has many uses, too. It rolls and spins. It can be used for bouncing as children sit on it in a ring and roll

off. Bill asked the teacher to hold it at the bottom of the slide and he came down and shot through the tube like a circus performer. It became a game in which most of the group joined. The tube can become a drum on which the children beat, setting up rhythm patterns with their hands. It is large and light and children find pleasure in using it in many ways.

Sound Making

Sound making articles have a place outdoors. Kegs with rubber stretched over the top make drums like the truck inner tube. A gong hung outside adds a sound experience and bells of many kinds such as cow bells may be used in "parades." The children themselves discover many unexpected sounds as they play where there is a variety of material available.

The Animal World

In outside play the children will also be exploring and discovering the world of plants and animals. We have mentioned making provisions for a garden. We also need to make provisions for keeping animals in the playground. Animals large and small, whose habits of living differ, give children the chance to broaden their concepts of the animal world. One school at different times kept twin lambs (raised on a bottle), a mother sheep and her lamb, a young goat, a large turtle (the only animal that ran away), ducks, hens and chickens, and rabbits. The bird, fish, tadpoles and white rats were "inside" animals. As visitors, this

school had kittens, puppies, a beautiful skunk, a bear cub, a fawn on his way to the park, and a little pig (who made a big hit with his squeal and his curly tail). The children never fail to become interested in the worms they discover in their digging. Many are the cans of worms collected in any school on a spring day after the ground is soft enough for digging. Caterpillars and cocoons are fascinating subjects of study. While observing a variety of animals and helping care for them, the children ask many questions and learn to feel at home with animals.

Part of the equipment of the play yard should consist of a well constructed animal cage where the smaller animals may be housed. A metal cage which can be easily cleaned and offers some kind of shelter, either with a cover or with a small box inside, makes a satisfactory way to care for a variety of animals. The larger animals are protected by the same fence that protects the children and they may find shelter in a shed. Living things have many lessons to teach young children.

Quiet Play Outside

Outdoor play is not always active and vigorous. When the weather is mild, much quiet play may go on outside. Most of what is done in the line of quiet play inside can also be carried on outside. Sometimes it can even go better outside. There is added freedom in finger painting done outdoors on a table with papers laid out to dry on the grass or pinned with clothes pins to a line. The easel can be set up out of the glare of direct sun-

"Do you know what? I can play a guitar, too."

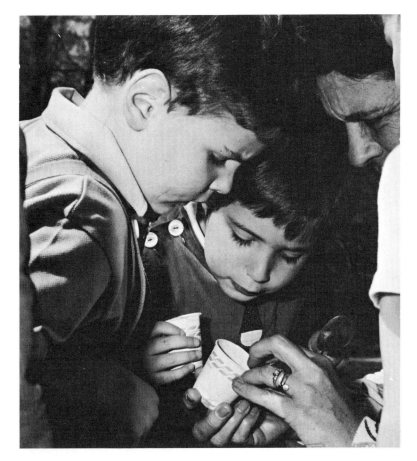

The easel can be set up out of the glare of direct sunlight.

The teacher answers questions, and leads the children toward newer discoveries.

light for easel painting. Soap bubbles sparkle in the sunshine. Clay used outdoors seems to bring more relaxation and stories are fun when told or read under a tree with the group on a blanket or a rug. There is more privacy for housekeeping play in the larger areas of the play yard and simple equipment made of orange crates, apple boxes, a table, a stove, a cabinet, chairs —can be kept outside if it is not desirable to move the indoor equipment outside. Doll babies need an airing in buggies. As long as the children are warm enough—and not too hot—they enjoy playing house outside.

Winter Sports

We have not spoken of "winter sports" perhaps because the outdoors is used more in warmer weather and seems to offer more pleasant possibilities then. Just because the possibilities are less apparent in cold weather the teacher's part may be of more importance. It may have to be the teacher who helps start a snowball and helps push it as it gets heavy and big. It is only the teacher who is strong enough to pull a group on a sled around the yard or give the sled a push down an incline. Taking hold of hands and running through the leaves in the fall is fun, but a quiet child may stand shivering until the teacher extends her hand and invites him with a smile to become active. Raking leaves with a bamboo rake or a broom made of twigs to clear the walks on the playground becomes a group project although the teacher may be the one who initiated it.

The teacher who enjoys outdoor play experiences and encourages children to enjoy them, needs to be dressed properly herself. The weather may call for warm socks, high boots, wool mittens and cap, maybe ski clothes if she is to stay outside. Her clothes should be as warm as the children's snow suits, or she will be likely to bring the group inside to meet her own need for warmth rather than theirs. The teacher who is not properly dressed for winter weather will find it hard to appreciate the possibilities in time spent outside. She will tend to limit the children's outdoor experiences.

THE TEACHER

Up to this point we have considered the space, the equipment and the activities possible outdoors. But the kind of contribution these things make to the development of the child depends in large part on the teacher. She (or he, in a few schools) is the key factor. She not only is responsible for selecting and adding to the equipment, rearranging it frequently, but she is largely responsible for the way it is used. The children must accept her values. If she can see the world through the eyes of a child, her playground will be a rich, exciting place, not always neat, but always full of satisfaction. She will enjoy being outside herself, and so will the children.

The teacher works *with* the children, facilitating, not interfering.

Enriching Experiences Rather Than Restricting

Since the well-equipped playground offers many possibilities for active play the children can be expected to play actively there. The teacher's role is not to limit and restrict. Rather it is to extend and enrich. She is there to see that there are many opportunities for active play and that these are varied, that they challenge different levels of group and individual interests. One child likes to build, another to ride the tricycle, another enjoys active dramatic play. Their interests shift. The teacher helps them all discover and carry on their own play while respecting the needs and purposes of others. She may at times need **to** encourage a shy, timid child, participating with him in an activity until he has built up enough assurance to play actively on his own. She may need to help an aggressive child channel his aggression, turning it into constructive uses or acceptable ones. Instead of annoying others, for example, the child may turn to digging or making an airplane or using the punching bag with her help. She works **with** the children, facilitating rather than interfering.

The teacher also opens new possibilities for learning. From her wider experience she enriches the play through suggestion and comment. She does not direct or organize play but, building on the children's spontaneous interests, she enlarges their horizons. She adds to their information about worms, for example, as they come upon a worm in their digging and ask questions. She may answer questions about plants or about the melting snow and the changing shadows on the walk. To answer the children's questions, to lead them toward new discoveries, to help them relate the unknown to what is already known is part of teaching, outside as well as inside. To teach in nursery school every teacher needs a background of knowledge in the physical and natural sciences. She must have facts and she herself must be curious if she is to further the intellectual development of children.

Careful Observation

If she is to contribute to the children's play in positive ways like these, the teacher must observe play carefully and constantly. It is easy to turn around and say "no" when the child starts to knock over a piece of equipment. An untrained person can do that! It takes an alert observer with sympathy and insight to understand what the child is trying to accomplish and suggest what he might do to carry out his purpose in an acceptable way. A trained teacher gives this kind of help and the child grows more adequate and confident because of it. Giving this help depends on observation and understanding. Sometimes one sees two teachers standing together on a playground absorbed in conversation about their adult concerns. They do not give attention to the children except when trouble arises. Or, one sees a teacher idle and bored looking outside. These people see their job as "child care," not teaching, for teaching is an active process —even though the activity may only be observation.

No need for quiet voices here!

Careful observation increases one's understanding of the children's individual needs so that one can be ready to step into situations with a suggestion that will meet the real needs of the children. Carrying a pencil and pad helps. Notes jotted down as one watches mean more penetrating observation and a record for later study.

The teacher who observes is not likely to step in and solve the children's problems for them. The teacher who watches can help the children find their own solutions because she understands what they are trying to do—and there is likely to be much problem solving in outdoor play—things too heavy, too high, too long, all to be dealt with!

Satisfactions Outside

Active play, problem solving play, explorations of the world, and sensory satisfactions, all are found outdoors. Teaching as a process is related to living experiences. Nowhere is it possible for children to live more fully than on a well planned and well equipped playground. Nowhere is good teaching more important or more satisfying. Let's go outdoors!

There is more privacy
for housekeeping play
in the larger places
of the play yard.

PURPOSES AND GOALS OF THE NATIONAL ASSOCIATION FOR THE EDUCATION OF YOUNG CHILDREN

The purpose of the National Association for the Education of Young Children, (nursery, kindergarten, primary) is to provide a medium for the advancement and development of sound group programs, focused on the well-being of young children under eight years of age. This was the stated goal of the National Association for Nursery Education, this organization's predecessor, since it was organized in 1931. Today's concept of early childhood education includes the nursery, kindergarten, and primary years as a psychological entity requiring consistency in the child's development of concepts, relationships, and positive attitudes toward himself and his achievements. This is essential preparation for the more organized school life to follow. It is recognized that these early years (under eight) are crucial, key years in the development of all persons.

The National Association for the Education of Young Children is the only national group concerned solely with the education of young children wherever they may be in group situations. Its publications and activities fill a need not now being met by any other group. The Association makes every effort, within the capabilities of its resources, to cooperate with other kindred organizations.

The National Association for the Education of Young Children aims to further public recognition of the significance of these early years of rapid growth and development by:

1. *Stimulating and coordinating the contributions of existing* separate yet related *organizations,* such as those concerned with children of migrant workers, child care centers, church sponsored groups, cooperative parent groups, handicapped children, and other groups at all socio-economic levels.

2. Offering skilled professional consultation and evaluation to publishers of children's books, toy manufacturers, architects designing children's premises and facilities, manufacturers of children's furniture, clothing and equipment, directors of children's T.V. and radio programs, and others providing materials for children.

3. Assisting individuals and a variety of groups working with and for young children through the stimulation of needed educational services and dissemination of information.

4. Serving young children through an expanded membership of workers at all levels and in all fields related to early childhood.

5. Promoting coordination and cooperation between agencies and departments concerned with children.

6. Developing sound objective national standards for group programs serving young children, assuring essential and adequate protection, yet allowing variety appropriate to particular situations.

7. Supporting legislative measures, whether local, state, or federal that will improve conditions for young children.